SURPRISINGLY SCARY!

Look Out for the MOSQUITO!

Maci Dessen

PowerKiDS press

New York

Published in 2016 by The Rosen Publishing Group, Inc.
29 East 21st Street, New York, NY 10010

Copyright © 2016 by The Rosen Publishing Group, Inc.

All rights reserved. No part of this book may be reproduced in any form without permission in writing from the publisher, except by a reviewer.

First Edition

Editor: Caitlin McAneney
Book Design: Katelyn Heinle

Photo Credits: Cover SW_Stock/Shutterstock.com; back cover, pp. 3, 4, 6, 8, 10–12, 14–16, 18, 20, 22–24 (background) CAMPINCOOL/Shutterstock.com; p. 5 Iurochkin Alexandr/Shutterstock.com; p. 7 Puneet Vikram Singh, Nature and Concept photographer/Moment Open/Getty Images; p. 9 (main) svr101/Shutterstock.com; p. 9 (map) ekler/Shutterstock.com; p. 11 (top) © iStockphoto.com/doug4537; p. 11 (bottom) Napat/Shutterstock.com; p. 13 Coprid/Shutterstock.com; p. 14 http://en.wikipedia.org/wiki/Yellow_fever#mediaviewer/File:Aedes_aegypti_bloodfeeding_CDC_Gathany.jpg; pp. 15 (vaccine), 16 BSIP/Universal Images Group Editorial/Getty Images; p. 15 (yellow fever virus) http://en.wikipedia.org/wiki/Yellow_fever#mediaviewer/File:YellowFeverVirus.jpg; p. 17 Leena Robinson/Shutterstock.com; p. 19 isifa/Getty Images News/Getty Images; p. 21 Paula Bronstein/Getty Images News/Getty Images; p. 22 ramshero/Shutterstock.com.

Library of Congress Cataloging-in-Publication Data

Dessen, Maci, author.
 Look out for the mosquito! / Maci Dessen.
     pages cm. — (Surprisingly scary!)
 Includes bibliographical references and index.
 ISBN 978-1-4994-0879-9 (pbk.)
 ISBN 978-1-4994-0900-0 (6 pack)
 ISBN 978-1-4994-0942-0 (library binding)
 1. Mosquitoes—Juvenile literature. I. Title. II. Series: Surprisingly scary!
 QL536.D47 2015
 595.77'2—dc23
                              2015006137

Manufactured in the United States of America

CPSIA Compliance Information: Batch #WS15PK: For Further Information contact Rosen Publishing, New York, New York at 1-800-237-9932

CONTENTS

Buzzing Beast 4
A Mosquito's Body 6
Mosquitoes Live Everywhere! 8
Mosquito Life Cycle 10
Bloodthirsty 12
Deadly Pests 14
West Nile Virus 16
Spreading Malaria 18
Stopping the Mosquito 20
The Tiniest Killer 22
Glossary 23
Index 24
Websites 24

Mosquitoes are common **insects** all over the word. There are more than 3,000 species, or kinds, of mosquitoes. These insects might look tiny, but they're huge pests. When mosquitoes bite, they leave an **itchy**, red bump. These bites are annoying, but can also be serious. Mosquitoes can spread many deadly **diseases** with their bites.

> When the weather's warm and wet, mosquitoes are often flying around for a bite!

SURPRISINGLY TRUE!

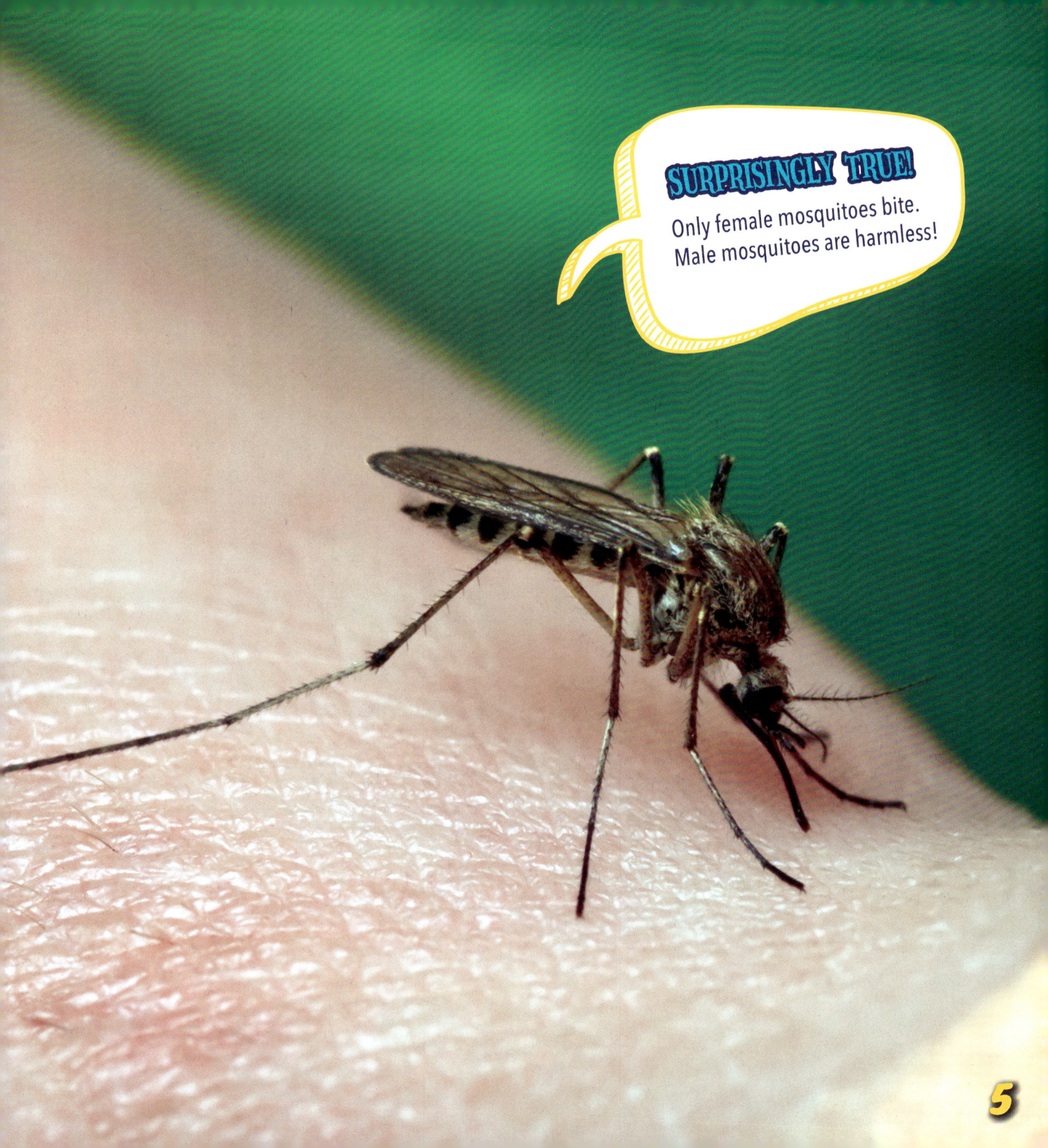

Only female mosquitoes bite. Male mosquitoes are harmless!

5

A MOSQUITO'S BODY

A mosquito's body is perfectly built to swoop through the air, find a **host**, and suck its blood. Its head has two big eyes that notice even the smallest movement. Mosquitoes have simpler eyes on the top of their head that notice changes in light.

Female mosquitoes have a mouthpart that's used to break a host's skin and suck out blood. Two long antennae, or feelers, can sense a person's breath from more than 100 feet (30 m) away!

> A mosquito's thorax has a pair of wings for flying and smaller winglike parts for changing direction. The abdomen holds the mosquito's stomach, which grows bigger as it drinks blood.

ANTENNAE

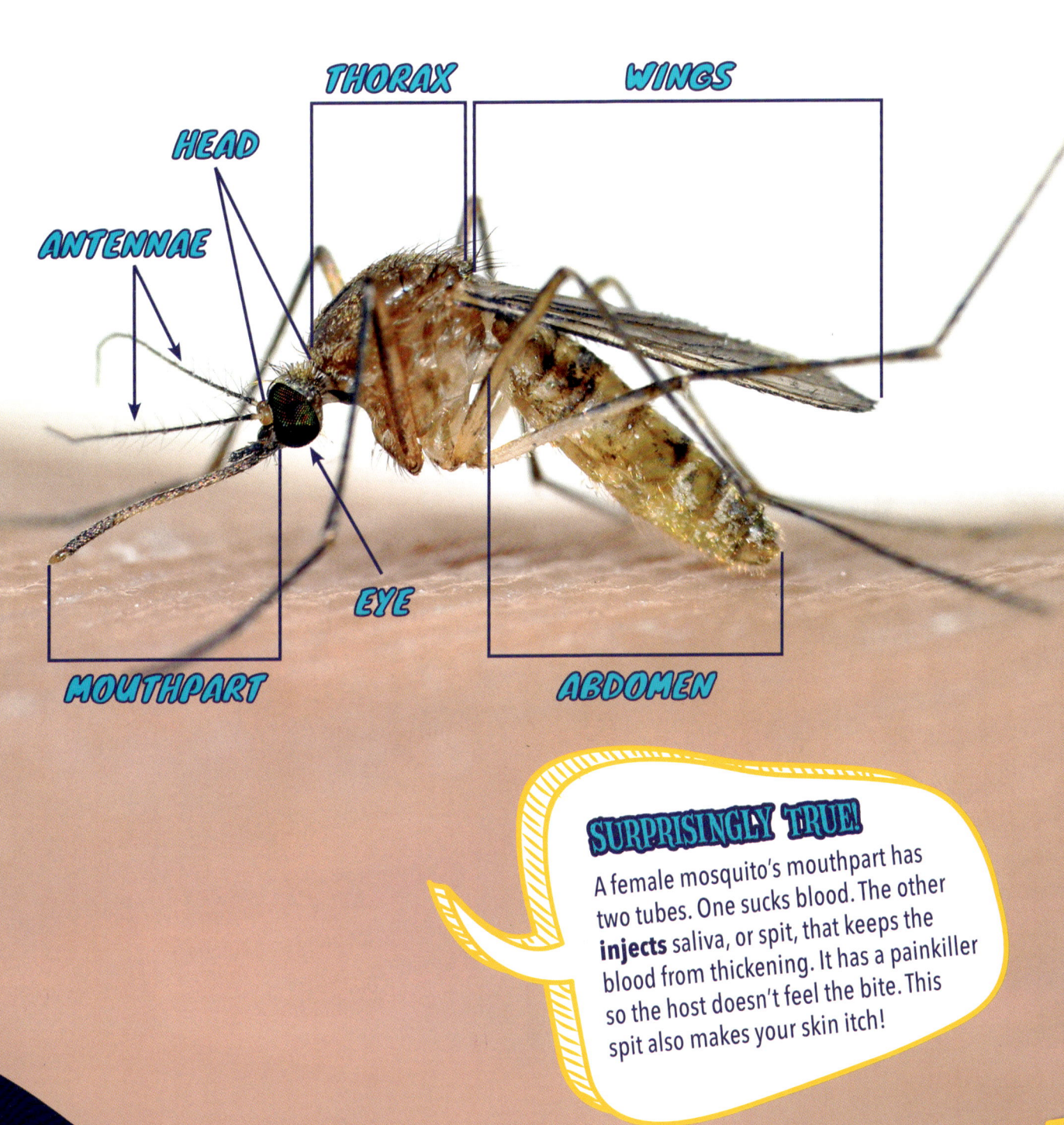

HEAD

THORAX

WINGS

EYE

MOUTHPART

ABDOMEN

SURPRISINGLY TRUE!

A female mosquito's mouthpart has two tubes. One sucks blood. The other **injects** saliva, or spit, that keeps the blood from thickening. It has a painkiller so the host doesn't feel the bite. This spit also makes your skin itch!

MOSQUITOES LIVE EVERYWHERE!

Mosquitoes are found throughout every continent on Earth except Antarctica. They prefer tropical areas, which are hot and wet. They're not too picky, though, and will settle for warm weather. Some even live in cold parts of the Arctic!

Mosquitoes are known to **infest** wetlands, or lands that have very wet soil or pools of water on top. That's because they lay eggs in stagnant, or still, water. Even a big puddle can be home to hundreds of mosquito eggs! Most mosquitoes don't mind dirty water, even if it's polluted.

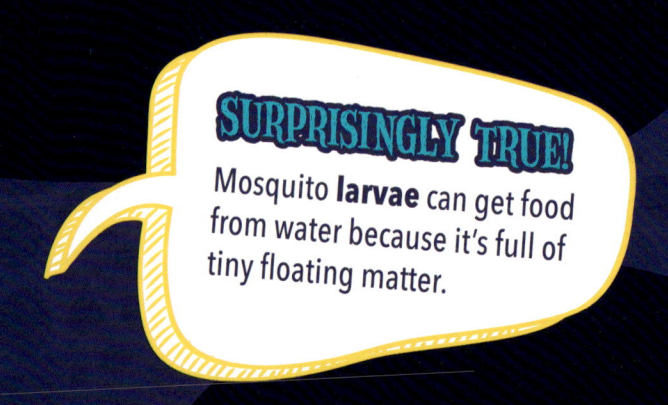

SURPRISINGLY TRUE!
Mosquito **larvae** can get food from water because it's full of tiny floating matter.

MOSQUITO TERRITORY

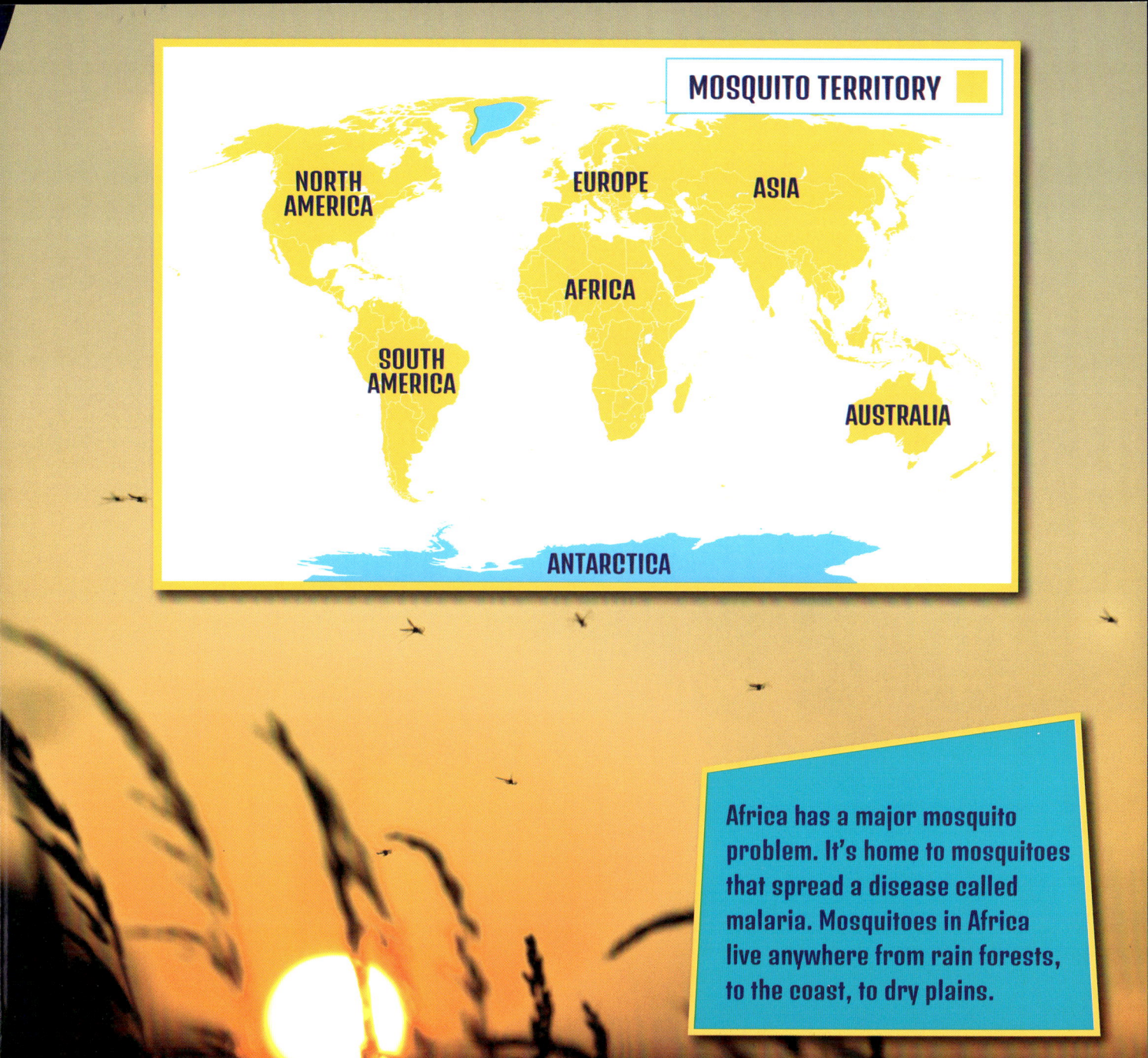

NORTH AMERICA · **EUROPE** · **ASIA** · **AFRICA** · **SOUTH AMERICA** · **AUSTRALIA** · **ANTARCTICA**

Africa has a major mosquito problem. It's home to mosquitoes that spread a disease called malaria. Mosquitoes in Africa live anywhere from rain forests, to the coast, to dry plains.

MOSQUITO LIFE CYCLE

How do these bloodsucking pests grow? First, a mother mosquito lays her eggs in still water. The eggs form a raft on the surface.

After about two days, a larva breaks out of its egg. The larva lives in the water and has a tail, but it comes to the surface for air. It eats tiny water-dwelling matter. A larva sheds its skin four times as it grows. Next, the larva turns into a pupa. It doesn't eat or move—it just rests and grows.

SURPRISINGLY TRUE!

One mosquito lays 100 eggs or more at a time! That's why mosquito populations are so high. Mosquitoes can live for two weeks to six months.

After its body has grown into an adult, the mosquito will break out of its skin one more time. An adult mosquito dries off and takes to the sky!

MOSQUITO LARVAE

BLOODTHIRSTY

Male mosquitoes are herbivores, or animals that eat only plant matter. They don't bother people or animals. They prefer to eat nectar, which is the sweet liquid in plants.

Female mosquitoes eat nectar, too. However, they're also thirsty for blood. This makes them omnivores, or animals that eat both plant and animal matter. Female mosquitoes drink blood to provide **nutrients** for their eggs. They prefer to drink the blood of horses, birds, and cows. However, if a tasty person comes along, they don't mind taking a bite!

> Mosquitoes usually come out to feed in the early morning or when the sun is setting.

SURPRISINGLY TRUE!

It seems that mosquitoes like to bite certain kinds of people, while they leave others alone. Scientists think it has something to do with how a person smells.

DEADLY PESTS

Each year, over 1 million people around the world die from illnesses carried by mosquitoes. Mosquitoes can pick up an illness from one person's blood and inject it into another person.

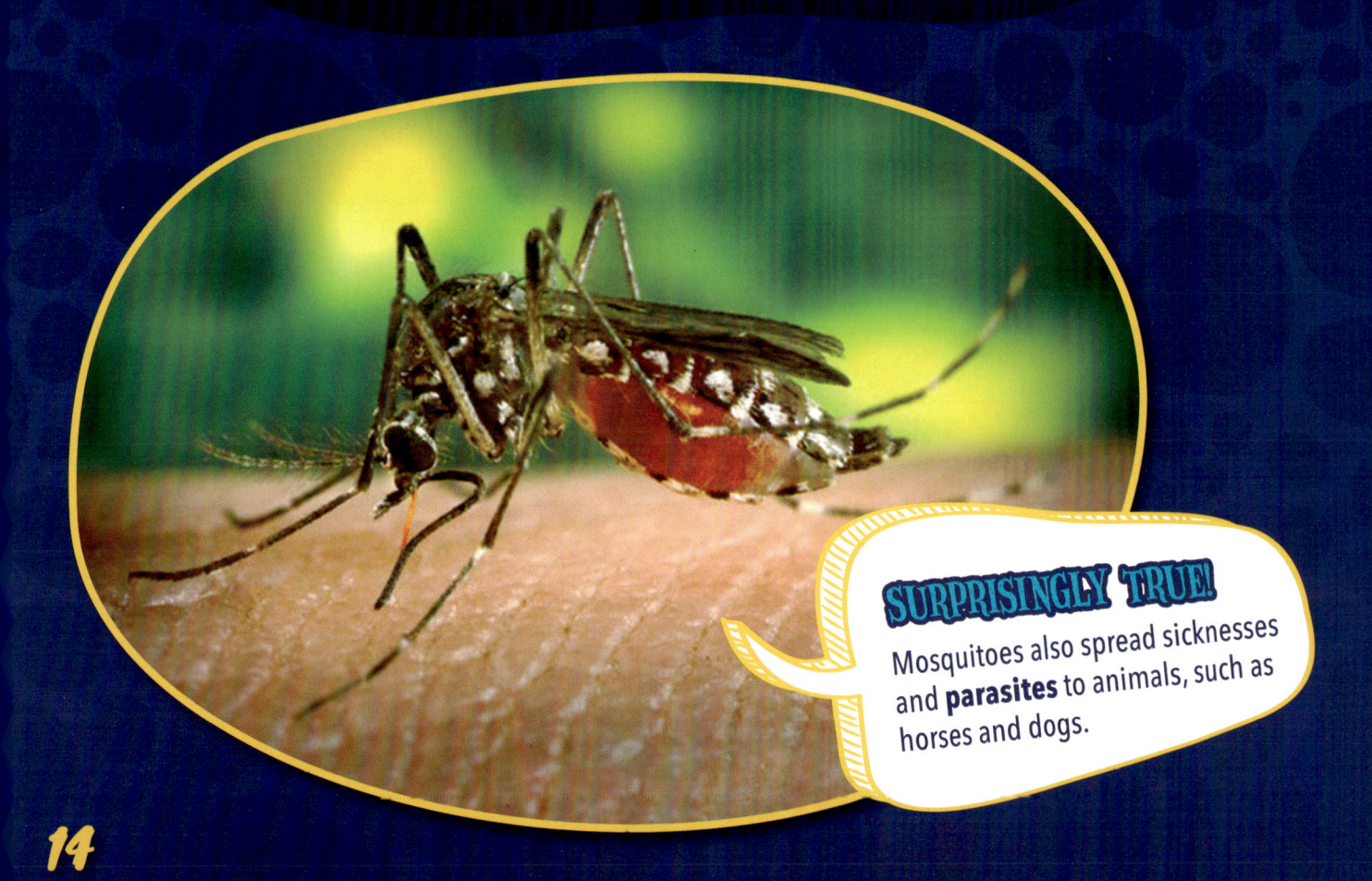

SURPRISINGLY TRUE!
Mosquitoes also spread sicknesses and **parasites** to animals, such as horses and dogs.

Mosquitoes spread yellow fever, which is a disease that causes fever, throwing up, bleeding, yellow skin, and often death. In 1793, yellow fever killed 5,000 people just in Philadelphia, Pennsylvania. Mosquitoes also spread dengue fever, which is a disease that causes fever, pain, headache, and sometimes death. Nearly 400 million people suffer from dengue fever every year.

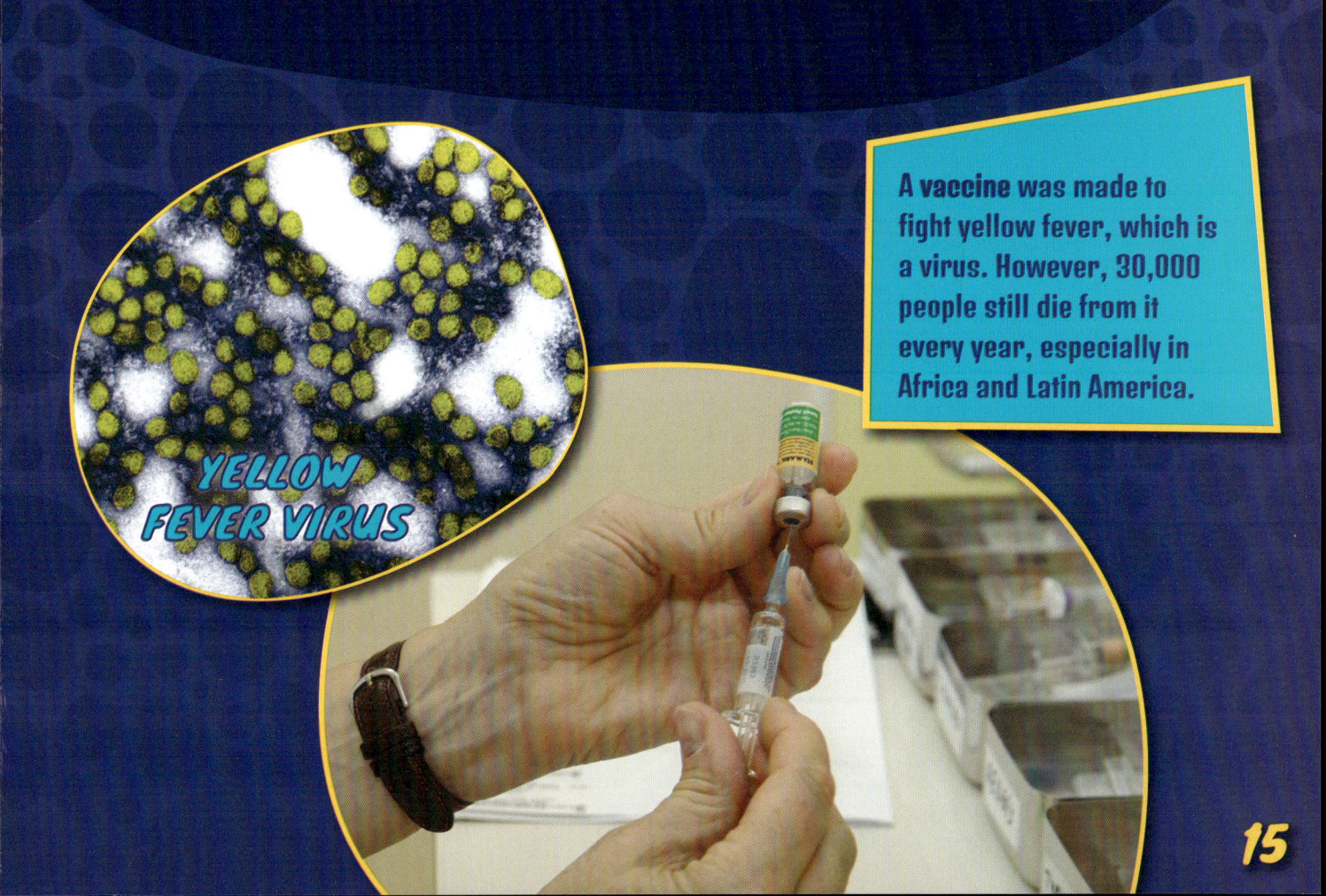

YELLOW FEVER VIRUS

A **vaccine** was made to fight yellow fever, which is a virus. However, 30,000 people still die from it every year, especially in Africa and Latin America.

Few people die from West Nile virus. However, a small number of infected people might get a serious brain disease that can take a long time to heal.

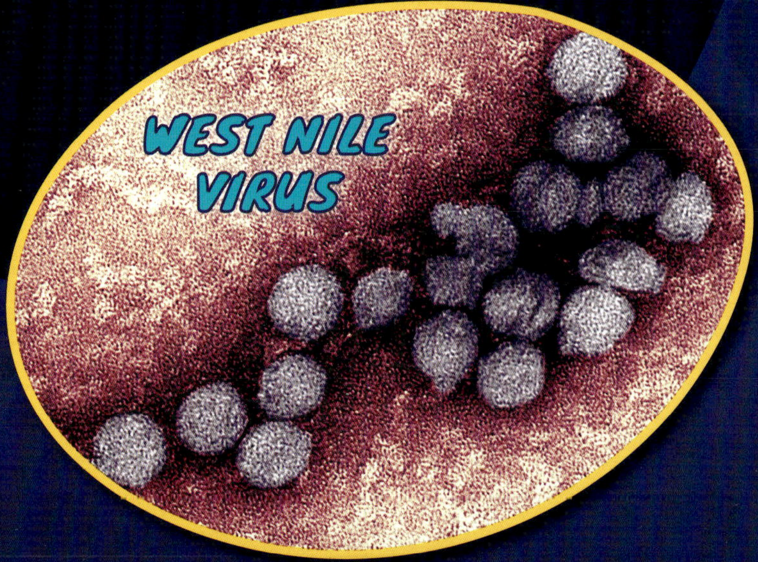

WEST NILE VIRUS

SURPRISINGLY TRUE!

West Nile virus has been found in 48 states in the United States.

MOSQUITOES ARE PRESENT IN THE AREA
WEAR LONG SLEEVES AND LONG PANTS
USE PROPER INSECT REPELLENT
TAKE EXTRA PRECAUTIONS AT DUSK AND DAWN

SPREADING MALARIA

Malaria is perhaps the most serious disease that's spread by mosquitoes. In 2010 alone, there were 219 million cases of malaria, resulting in 660,000 deaths. Most malaria deaths occur in Africa. However, about 1,500 cases are found in the United States each year.

People who've been bitten by a malaria-infected mosquito usually see symptoms in 7 to 30 days. Infected people start to suffer from fever, sweating, chills, headaches, and throwing up. This parasite-caused disease can be treated if it's caught quickly.

> If malaria can be treated, why do people die? Malaria is common in African countries that are poor and unable to carry out plans to prevent or treat the disease.

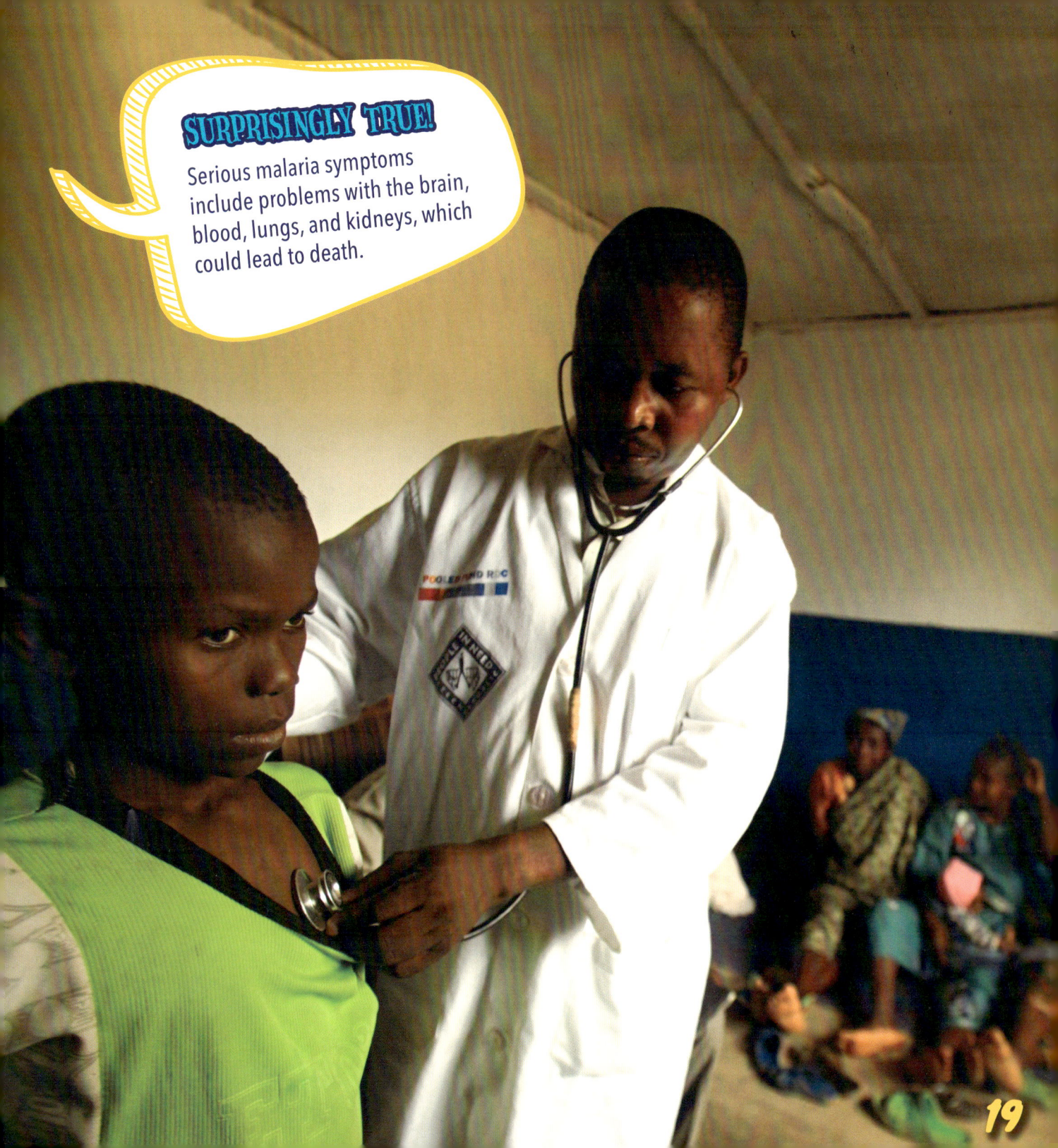

SURPRISINGLY TRUE!
Serious malaria symptoms include problems with the brain, blood, lungs, and kidneys, which could lead to death.

19

STOPPING THE MOSQUITO

Mosquito-spread illnesses may seem unstoppable. However, there are ways people can decrease their chances of being bitten.

First, wear long sleeves and pants when you're outside, especially if it's the early morning or at sunset. Wear mosquito repellent, which is a spray or cream you put on your skin to keep mosquitoes away. If you're sleeping outside, use a special mosquito net to keep the pests away. Many mosquito nets have mosquito repellent on them.

SURPRISINGLY TRUE!

Mosquitoes love still water, remember? To decrease mosquitoes where you live, get rid of still water in buckets, puddles, and ditches.

These children in Cambodia rest underneath a mosquito net. Cambodia suffers from a kind of malaria that can't be treated by drugs, so these nets are important.

THE TINIEST KILLER

The only good thing about mosquitoes is that some animals, such as bats and dragonflies, rely on them for food. In fact, bringing bats into a mosquito-rich area can decrease the mosquito population quickly.

The tiny mosquito might be the world's most powerful killer. Mosquito populations grow quickly, and their bites can carry parasites and viruses. Scientists and doctors are still looking for ways to stop this bloodthirsty bug in its tracks.

GLOSSARY

disease: Illness.

host: A living thing that another living thing lives or feeds on.

infect: To spread germs from one thing to another.

infest: To overrun a place in large numbers and become harmful or unpleasant.

inject: To force something into the body.

insect: A small creature that has three body parts, six legs, and often has wings.

itchy: Producing an unpleasant feeling on your skin that makes you want to scratch.

larvae: Bugs in an early life stage that have a wormlike form. The singular form is "larva."

nutrient: Something taken in by a plant or animal that helps it grow and stay healthy.

parasite: A living thing that lives in, on, or with another living thing and often harms it.

vaccine: A shot that keeps a person from getting a certain sickness.

INDEX

A
abdomen, 6, 7
Africa, 9, 15, 16, 18
antennae, 6, 7

B
bats, 22

D
dengue fever, 15
diseases, 4, 9, 15, 16, 18
dragonflies, 22

E
eggs, 8, 10, 12
eyes, 6, 7

F
female mosquitoes, 5, 6, 7, 10, 12

L
larvae, 8, 10, 11

M
malaria, 9, 18, 19, 21
male mosquitoes, 5, 12
mosquito net, 20, 21
mosquito repellent, 20
mouthpart, 6, 7

N
nectar, 12

P
parasites, 14, 18, 22

S
still water, 8, 20

T
thorax, 6, 7

V
virus, 15, 16, 22

W
West Nile virus, 16, 17

Y
yellow fever, 15

WEBSITES

Due to the changing nature of Internet links, PowerKids Press has developed an online list of websites related to the subject of this book. This site is updated regularly. Please use this link to access the list: www.powerkidslinks.com/surp/mosq